With love to our little angel, Zach
~ Mimi

THE WISE ANIMAL HANDBOOK

Kate B. Jerome

ARCADIA KIDS

Attempt new skills from time to time.

Just **try** to think them **through.**

And if you **find** you're left behind...

...then change your point of view.

Try not to think of just yourself.

Invent new ways to share.

Stay close to friends whom you can trust.

But
always
be
aware.

Avoid
the
tattle
in the
tale.

Insist that **truth** is **best.**

Embrace with pride the strengths you have.

Demand
to be
impressed.

Enjoy the peace that nature brings.

Ignore what's just for show.

Join **forces** when
the road gets **rough.**

Admit when you don't know.

Remember **family** is the **best.**

Despite the ups and downs.

Don't **hide** from things that you must **face.**

Make
joyful
laughing
sounds.

Eat **healthy** food to **grow** up **strong.**

Be **patient** with your friends.

Try not to take a stubborn stand.

Be
quick
to make
amends.

Excuse yourself when manners slip.

Be **helpful** every **day.**

Keep trying even when it's hard.

But
don't
forget to
play!

And
sing

...and **dance** each **day!**

Written by Kate B. Jerome
Design and Production: Lumina Datamatics, Inc.
Coloring Illustrations: Tom Pounders
Research: Eric Nyquist

Cover Images: See back cover

Interior Images: 002 Anetapics/Shutterstock.com; 003 George Green/Shutterstock.com; 004 Sergey
Uryadnikov/Shutterstock.com; 005 Gnomeandi/Shutterstock.com; 006 Bruce MacQueen/Shutterstock.com;
007 Henk Bentlage/Shutterstock.com; 008 M.M./Shutterstock.com; 009 Mikael Damkier/Shutterstock.com; 010
Brendan van Son/Shutterstock.com; 011 Michael Pettigrew/Shutterstock.com; 012 StevenRussellSmithPhotos/
Shutterstock.com; 013 Pakhnyushchy/Shutterstock.com; 014 Patjo/Shutterstock.com; 015 Quinn Martin/
Shutterstock.com; 016 Lincoln Rogers/Shutterstock.com; 017 Dirk Ercken/Shutterstock.com; 018 Karel Gallas/
Shutterstock.com; 019 Orangecrush/Shutterstock.com; 020 Guenter-foto/Shutterstock.com; 021 Janecat/
Shutterstock.com; 022 Shironina/Shutterstock.com; 023 Annette Shaff/Shutterstock.com; 024 Vitaly
Titov/Shutterstock.com; 025 Rohappy/Shutterstock.com; 026 MattiaATH/Shutterstock.com; 027 Otsphoto/
Shutterstock.com; 028 FikMik/Shutterstock.com; 029 Four Oaks/Shutterstock.com; 030 Ekaterina Kolomeets/
Shutterstock.com; 031 Hugh Lansdown/Shutterstock.com.

Published by Arcadia Kids, a division of Arcadia Publishing and
The History Press, Charleston, SC

For all general information contact Arcadia Publishing at:
Telephone: 843-853-2070
Email: sales@arcadiapublishing.com

For Customer Service and Orders:
Toll Free: 1-888-313-2665
Visit us on the Internet at www.arcadiapublishing.com

Library of Congress Cataloging-in-Publication data is on file with the publisher.

Printed in China

Texas State Insect

Monarch Butterfly

Read Together

The monarch butterfly was named the state insect in 1995. You can find monarch butterflies traveling through Texas in the fall and spring.

Texas State Large Mammal
Longhorn

Read Together

The vote for state animal was a tie between the longhorn and the 9-banded armadillo. So in 1995, Texas officials decided the longhorn would be the state's large mammal and the armadillo would be the state's small mammal!

Texas State **Small Mammal**

Nine-Banded Armadillo

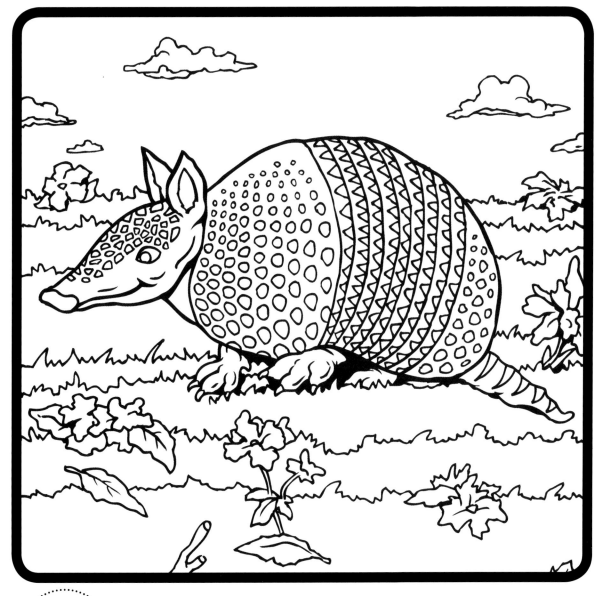

© Kate B. Jerome 2017

Read Together

The nine-banded armadillo was named the state small mammal in 1995. These little animals sometimes jump straight up into the air when they are startled!

Texas State Bird

Mockingbird

Read Together

The mockingbird was named the state bird of Texas in 1927 after a request from the Texas Federation of Women's Clubs. This amazing little bird can sing so well that it's nicknamed the "King of Song."